THE SKELETON SUTRAS

Rob Plath

Epic Rites Press

First edition.
Printed in the USA.

Editor: Wolfgang Carstens
Exterior Art and Design: Yvette
Sohl

ISBN: 978-1-926860-55-8

www.epicrites.org

A HAPPY SKELETON

There was a skeleton that was a
face painter in the city. He was
sad most of the time, but when
he painted peoples' faces, he
became a happy skeleton. He sat
on a milk crate on the corner
with a sign SKELETON FACE
PAINTER. He didn't use sparkles
or bright colors. In fact, he
only used black and white. Armed
with a sponge and a brush the
bony fingers transformed grown-
up's faces and children's faces
into big or little skulls. And
as all the other heavy human
faces moved about in the streets
of the city, pressing their lips
tightly together, narrowing
their eyes and wrinkling their
brows, these skull faces floated
around, peacefully beneath the
sun, stretching their smiles.

A SKELETON'S DREAM

The skeleton was bored in his
crypt. To pass the time he'd
count his ribs over and over or
he'd open and close his jaws so
his teeth chattered like he was
performing some kind of crazy
skeleton exercise in eternity.
The sound made him sweetly
recall the way teeth clicked
during a wild, reckless kiss.
Then he thought of the stars.
I'm bored in here, but if I
could look up at the stars I'd
be okay, he thought. I'd endure
this existence if the stars were
visible. I wouldn't have to play
these games with my ribs or
jaws. I'd just look up at those
silver pinpoints of light and
peacefully dream away in the
forever darkness.

ACQUAINTED WITH THE BLUES

There was a melancholy skeleton elephant that walked alone in the wilderness trying to escape her sadness, her heavy gait full of pain. She left deep tracks in the earth like fossils of agony. One day, exhausted, she came upon a small hill and sat down. She sat and sat with her burden. At some point a bone bird landed on a stone besides her. You have such wonderful blue tusks, the bone bird said. I've never seen blue tusks before. They make me want to sing sad songs. The melancholy skeleton elephant turned her eyes downward, realizing her tusks had turned blue. The bone bird began to sing from the stone. The melancholy skeleton elephant loved the song so much that she raised her blue tusks like great horns made out of the sky and let out a solemn wail that made the stars tip their silver hats.

THE SAD BONE-BUTTERFLY

Once while aimlessly flitting
about a sad bone-butterfly
discovered a baby bull-skeleton
weeping in a field. "Why are you
crying," inquired the sad bone-
butterfly. "I was playing and I
lost my heart," said the baby
bull-skeleton and he continued
to cry. "That's sad," lamented
the sad bone-butterfly and flew
down and perching itself on the
baby bull-skeleton's muzzle
began to drink its tears. "Thank
you," said the baby bull-
skeleton. Then the bone-
butterfly placed the crimson
face of a hibiscus flower inside
his ribcage and suddenly the
baby bull-skeleton began to romp
around, happily kicking its hind
bone-legs. "I bet you can't
catch me," the bone-butterfly
mischievously teased, flapping
her bone-wings above his now
tearless muzzle and the baby
bull-skeleton chased the bone-
butterfly over the hills for
days and days and they were both
very happy.

THE WIND THROUGH THE BOUGHS

The sad skeleton was sick of being cramped in a box inside a vault, so with all his might he pressed his bone-palms against the sides of his coffin until it collapsed and then pushed the hinges of the crypt door open and ran happily on his bone-heels into the night. But all the gravestones made him yawn, reminding him too much of his tomb. Walking a while through the rows he came upon an oak. *How beautiful the bare branches look against the midnight blue sky*! he said. It was then he decided to climb it. Settling on a sturdy bough about halfway up, the skeleton felt inseparable from his new home, grinning whenever the wind blew through his ribs.

BONE MUSIC

He fasted until his ribs
surfaced. Out of boredom and
curiosity, he took a tablespoon
and ran it along one row of
bones. The sound made him grin.
"Ah, my own music at last," he
said. All the meaty people had
no music inside of them, he
thought. They were too busy and
greedy. They were very far away
from their music and probably
would never find it. So he set
down a milk crate on the
sidewalk and there he sat with
his spoons and a slab of
cardboard at his feet that had
written on it: Bone Music. At
first, people stopped every now
and then to listen to the
strange, charming sounds. But
every day he fasted, the music
became clearer and more
beautiful. The bars of his ribs
were like magic xylophones. Soon
people gathered every day. Once
he thought he saw the ghost of
the great composer Shostakovich
smiling among the crowd.

MELANCHOLY SKELETON-MERMAID

There once was a melancholy
skeleton-mermaid with long hair
the color of orange lilies and
bones the color of lavender and
even though she was full of
mourning, she sang the most
beautiful songs. Upon hearing
her sorrowful notes, skeletons
of fish in the sea were brought
to life. As she sang from her
azure rocks, countless bone-fish
from deep beneath surfaced and
you could see their bone-fins
circling the melancholy
skeleton-mermaid and as long as
she continued to sing, each
bone-fish, one after the other,
leaped over her in an arc and
back into the sea.

A SKELETON'S TALE

The skeleton was sad. He lived
in a crypt on fire. Although he
was all bones, he owned a heart.
His heart had adapted to the
flames, but he feared someday
it'd turn into smoke. Some
nights when the fire died down
he'd take his heart from behind
his ribs, cup it in his bone
hands and talk to it. I won't
let you turn to smoke, he'd say.
One day there won't be any walls
to hold us. One day we'll lie in
a green field and there'll be
tall grass instead of flames.
One day the only heat will be
from the faraway sun. One day
I'll grow skin and you'll live
in cool shade and we'll sleep on
clover beneath the moon. Then
he'd place his heart back behind
his ribs and endure the fire.

THE LONE BIRCH AND THE SAD SKELETON

The sad skeleton had such a heavy heart in life that it remained with him after it ended. It was a great, red weight haunting his core. The other skeletons teased him and called him a freak and when witching hour arrived and they all left their plots to dance and leap over stones, they did not let him join in. Jealously he watched from afar, listening to them laugh their bone-laughter as the night breeze blew through the empty cages of their ribs. Finally wandering into the windy shadows, the sad skeleton rested his bones beneath a lone birch that sweetly murmured to his swollen heart.

THE SAD SKELETON-FAIRY

There once was a sad skeleton-
fairy that flew around night
after night, flapping her bone
wings and crying. One night when
the moon was full she was drawn
to a very solemn sound. She
landed on a birch branch just
above a large spiral shell on
the ground below. "Hello?" the
skeleton-fairy whispered. A
ghost-snail raised its head and
looked up at her. "Hello," it
answered. "What are you doing?"
asked the skeleton-fairy. "I'm
haunting my shell," the ghost-
snail replied. "You have a
beautiful shell," the skeleton-
fairy said. "Thank you," said
the ghost-snail. Then the ghost-
snail heard a ticking noise on
its shell. It was the fairy's
tears that were solid as grains
of sand. "Why are you crying?"
asked the ghost-snail. The
skeleton-fairy answered, "I'm
very sad." "I'm very sad too and
I'm sick of haunting my shell,"
said the ghost-snail, "Let's go
somewhere." So the sad ghost-
snail and the sad skeleton-fairy
both flew side by side through
the night. After a long time
they came upon something
magnificent—a city of dried,
black sunflowers. They were tall
as small trees with all their
heads bowed in the moonlight and
their dark, raggedy crowns all
hummed collectively like monks.
The skeleton-fairy and the
ghost-snail smiled for the first

time in what seemed like ages.
As they flew closer above the
dead sunflower city beneath the
moon, the humming grew louder,
welcoming both of them.

SKELETON BOY

Skeleton boy sitting in the
rain—rows of drops hanging from
his ribcage. Skeleton boy
sitting in the rain—beads
rolling down the buttons of his
spine. Skeleton boy sitting in
the rain—his neck bent, his
skull resting on his bone-fists,
daydreaming.

AT THE BACK OF THE CEMETERY

The sad skeleton was walking
around at the back of the
cemetery one stormy evening when
he saw something high up in an
oak. The sad skeleton scaled the
tree and saw it was a kite
caught in the branches. A blue
octopus! he laughed. His bone-
digits quickly untangled the
string and he descended. Then
the sad skeleton ran along the
avenues of the dead with the
kite and eventually the octopus
climbed into the wind. You're
free my friend! he yelled and
his skull opened up into a wide
smile at the way the blue
tentacles danced beneath the
steel-colored clouds.

THE LOTUS SKELETON

The sad skeleton was bored with
his fellow skeletons. All the
others did was either lie in
their crypts or run around the
rows of stones at witching hour,
rattling their bones, scaring
the shit out of the living. They
were either dull or mean. It was
then that the skeleton decided
to get some rich pink paint and
draw lotus flowers all over his
bones. After he was covered in
lotuses, he walked around the
city. Everywhere he went, people
stopped and their skin stretched
into smiles and they seemed to
forget their ancient fear. His
bone-heels continued down the
city sidewalks even after dark.
And for those lucky enough to
witness the stars above and the
lotus skeleton below, the night
was bearable.

THE BONE-FISH

The sad skeleton-cat crept on tiny bone-feet down the alleyway, weaving in and out of the garbage cans when it came upon an overturned pail. Among the ugly debris there was a beautiful bone-fish. The sad skeleton-cat picked up the bone-fish in its mouth and carried it down the dark streets to a small pond in the park. There the skeleton-cat dropped the bone-fish into the water. The bone-fish rested on its side for a few moments then suddenly flipped over and began to swim. The sad skeleton-cat smiled a wide grin watching the bone-fin dart through the reflection of the moon.

MAGIC PURPLE FIRE

When the sad skeleton was
melancholy and yearning for the
old days of skin he'd take a
walk and gently recline upon the
buttons of his spine in a very
large lavender patch just
outside the cemetery. He liked
how some of the lavender spikes
rose up through his frame and
how fat bumblebees hummed from
flower to flower above his
ribcage. Then a long sigh would
arise out of his skull and the
scent of the lavender would
bring on sweet crazy dreams as
his bones lay at the center of
the magic purple fire.

THE FIRST SNOW

The sad skeleton was moping
around until he happened to gaze
out of his little crypt window.
"Ah, the first snow," he sighed.
After a while the snow slowed to
a few flakes and the sad
skeleton thought of his boyhood
and happily decided to leave his
crypt. In front of each stone
the sad skeleton lay down on his
back and flapped his bone-arms
and moved his bone-legs in and
out. Then he returned satisfied
to his tomb. And when the
visitors arrived they smiled and
some wept at the snow angels
shining in the sun down the
avenues of the dead.

SELF-PORTRAIT

The sad skeleton was roaming
around the deserted alleyways
one night when he found a fat
piece of chalk. He sat there
with the knobs of his spine
against a brick wall thinking of
what he could create with the
dusty white stick. Then the sad
skeleton decided to draw a self-
portrait. After a while he
finished and stepped back a few
paces and gazed at his work. It
was a skeleton lying on its side
with its right hand supporting
its skull like a sleeping
Buddha. The skull looked as if
it were smiling. Just then a
beat-up looking cat appeared. It
paused and then slinked by. He
decided to take the last nub of
chalk and add a cat with a
missing ear next to the sleeping
Buddha skeleton. As he walked
back to the cemetery the clouds
shifted exposing the moon and
the chalk dust clinging to the
wall was aglow.

DOWNWARD DOG

The sad skeleton was super blue,
so he left his gloomy tomb and
walked out beneath the birches.
Standing beneath the boughs the
sad skeleton decided to practice
yoga. After sitting cross-
legged, he went into downward
dog pose. His bone-digits spread
out pressing against the earth
and his tail-bone pointed
skyward. It felt great to bend
his stiff frame. That's when the
skeleton-cat arrived. The
skeleton-cat was very excited
and kept rubbing against his
leg-bones and nudging the sad
skeleton's skull with its bone-
snout. The sad skeleton's jaw
stretched into a smile and his
ribcage lightly shook for the
first time in weeks. Then in the
yellow light of the moon the
skeleton-cat curled up, humming
beneath the triangular-shaped
bone-arch the sad skeleton's
shape made.

EMPTY SPACES

Late one evening the sad
skeleton walked out of the
cemetery gates and wandered the
avenues of the living. At the
end of one long road there was a
house being built. The sad
skeleton stood at the center of
all the studs and joists. He
thought of all of the
forthcoming walls and
rectangular doors and then
decided to hoist himself up into
the rafters. Once perched up
there, the sad skeleton sat
carelessly kicking his legs back
and forth gazing at the stars as
the cool wind blew straight
through all the empty spaces.

FIGURE 8s

Sad skeleton boy riding his
ancient bicycle up and down the
avenues of the dead. Sad
skeleton boy with yellow leaves
trailing out of his torn basket.
Sad skeleton boy making figure
8s around illegible stones, the
spokes turning and turning in
the moonlight.

PAPER LANTERNS

One winter afternoon the sad
skeleton was sick of his dreary
crypt. Just because it's a crypt
doesn't mean it has to be
dreary, he thought. He sat on
top of his coffin, kicking his
feet, thinking. Then suddenly he
jumped down on his bone-heels
and shouted, paper lanterns! For
hours his bone-digits snipped
the shapes of two-dozen
lanterns—blue ones, orange ones,
yellow ones, green ones and
white ones. When he was
finished, he strung the paper
lanterns and the sad skeleton
was delighted how they floated
wall-to-wall, gently perforating
grand openings in the
dreariness.

THE LINES OF THE LEAVES

The sad skeleton heard the crew
arrive with terrible tools to
destroy the silence and chew up
the poor, fallen leaves. What
was a graveyard without the
beauty of the leaves? he
thought. So the sad skeleton
decided to chase the leaf
killers away. He made his best
scary skull-face and ran out of
the crypt howling like a madman
and jumping from stone to stone,
rattling his bones. The men's
jaws dropped and they ran to
their truck and zoomed away,
leaving the sad skeleton
grinning in a cloud of dust. The
sad skeleton knew the leaf
killers would be back
eventually, so he gathered as
many leaves as his bone-arms
could carry and piled them in
his crypt. The sad skeleton was
overjoyed by the earthy scent of
the leaves that now replaced the
musty smell of the tomb. That
night the sad skeleton climbed
into his coffin and happily lay
there, examining the lines of
the leaves by holding them up
against the face of the moon
that shone through the little
crypt window.

THE SKELETON UNICORN

The skeleton unicorn stood
achingly upon her bone-hooves in
a bright field. She was frowning
when she noticed a bone-
caterpillar inching along her
horn. "Why aren't you climbing
on flowers?" she inquired.
"Flowers reject me," the
caterpillar sighed. "I
understand. I'm a skeleton
unicorn," she lamented. "Who
ever heard of a skeleton
unicorn?" The caterpillar
wiggled down to her bone-snout.
"We should go for a walk." The
unicorn agreed. After a long
while they came to a clearing.
They were on the edge of what
appeared to be a graveyard. Bone
dogs and bone cats happily
chased each other around stones.
Skeleton birds glided over plots
and bone rabbits leapt through
the rows. "It's an animal
cemetery," exclaimed the
caterpillar. They stood
absorbing the joy before them.
"Look," said the unicorn. It was
a large garden. Bone faces of
flowers smiled upon long stems
like spinal columns beneath the
beautiful grey cloudland.

THE HUM WITHIN

One cold evening a stray cat slinked into the crypt where the sad skeleton lived. The skeleton, who was sitting on top of his coffin, said, "I don't have any meat for you, but I can scratch behind your ears" and his jaws opened into a bone-smile. After circling the coffin several times, the cat jumped into his lap and as promised he scratched behind its ears with his bone-digits. Later, after the sleepy skeleton lay down for the night, the kitty accepted his invitation to curl up inside his ribcage, filling the crypt with a gentle, steady humming.

MUSIC IN THE ALLEYWAY

The skeleton yawned and leapt
from his crusty crypt and
decided to walk around one
night. In an alleyway, the
skeleton came upon an old
typewriter sitting on a crate in
the moonlight. He took his long
bone finger and jabbed a key and
clack went the typewriter. He
hit some more keys. Click,
clack, click, clack went the old
machine beneath the moon… He
walked around and found an old
flyer stapled to a pole and tore
it off. He fed the flyer into
the roller so the blank side
wound through and faced him.
This time he used all ten of his
bone fingers. When he was
finished he tore out the page.
It read: "Don't neglect the
flowers!" and "Be kind to
animals!" The skeleton smiled
briefly reminiscing about his
beloved cat and the little
garden he had when he was alive
and then tacked his messages to
the wooden pole. He found
another expired flyer and once
again his skull floated over the
old machine in the moonlight.
Through the wee hours of the
night the otherwise silent
alleyway was alive with the
strange music.

THE LONELY BONE-TREE

All the trees in the forest wore
thick bark and were bursting
with leaves or needles and a
countless amount held the nests
of animals, except for the
lonely bone-tree. It stood
alone, bleach-white and bare.
Even the creatures of the night,
the bats and the owls, preferred
trees that showed some signs of
life and the bone-tree couldn't
help but be envious of all the
other trees. Then one night a
full moon cast its light and in
it grew the shadow of a snail.
In the glow of the moonlight its
spiral was dazzling. It was the
most beautiful snail in the land
and upon seeing the lonely bone-
tree, it decided to slide up the
spine-trunk to rest on a bone-
limb and in the bone-boughs the
most beautiful snail in the land
fell asleep and had blissful
dreams. At dawn, the snail
glided down to continue on its
journey and the bone-tree was
very sad to see its only guest
ever depart. An unknown amount
of time went by and the most
beautiful snail in the land
returned with a long trail of
other quite striking snails and
one-by-one, they glided up the
bone-tree's spine-trunk and the
dazzling spirals filled its
bone-boughs and the bone-tree
felt joy all the way down to its
bone-roots and all the other
trees in the forest were
envious.

TEMPORARILY CALM FLESH

It was January and everything
was extra dead in the cemetery.
The sad skeleton yawned and
feeling bored wandered into the
old chapel. Drawn to a jar on a
crooked shelf, his bone digits
fished out a thin stick within
the glass and lifted it to his
bone nose-holes. Rose! He
excitedly left with matches and
incense sticks. You could see
his bones dancing down the
avenues of the dead, smoke
trailing behind him. Not long
after the sad skeleton returned
to his crypt, a few mourners
arrived. As they stood before
the stone, lingering ghostly
wisps of rose transformed their
shivering pinched faces into
temporarily calm flesh.

THE TERRIBLE GLASS

The sad skeleton wandered into
an abandoned house and
discovered a rabbit suspended in
solution in a jar on a shelf. He
gazed into its petrified eyes.
Poor rabbit! He thought of the
tormented poet whose sadness
made her feel like she was
suffocating beneath a bell-
shaped glass. It was then he
decided to name the rabbit
Sylvia. You're coming with me,
Sylvia, he said, taking the jar
in his bone-hands. He walked a
long time until he came to a
clearing in the woods beside a
lake. With his bone-digits he
dug and dug until he had an
acceptable-sized hole. At last
the sad skeleton lifted her out
of the terrible glass and rested
the loose body in the earth.
Before pushing the soil back in
again, he put leaves over her.
When he finished, the sad
skeleton said, May butterflies
rise from your grave each year,
and then he walked back to his
crypt.

COUNTING PETALS

The sad skeleton took his daily
stroll down the avenues of the
dead. After a long time of
walking he decided to lie down
in his favorite spot beneath the
cherry blossom tree. The bright
fallen blossoms made a wide
circle around the trunk and the
sad skeleton lay within it
counting the pink petals that
gently floated down. When at
last the moon rose he drowsily
walked back to his crypt with
the glowing confetti stuck to
his bones.

ABOUT ROB PLATH

Rob Plath is a 46-year-old
writer from New York. Rob has
written over a dozen books. He
lives with his cat and is a
vegan. Check out his website
robplath.com.

BOOKS BY ROB PLATH

Ashtrays and Bulls (Liquid Paper
Press 2003)
An IV Bag Full Of Bile
(Scintillating Publications
2007)
Whiskey and Clay (Pudding House
Publications 2008)
*Squeezing Blood From The
Alphabet* (Erbacce Press 2008)
Tapping Ashes In The Dark
(Lummox Press 2008)
*There's A Little Hobo In My
Heart Who Forever Gives The
Finger To Humanity*
(D/e/a/d/b/e/a/t Press 2008)
*Nicotine Scribblings From A
Hammock In The Void* (Good Japan
Press 2009)
A Bellyful of Anarchy (Epic
Rites Press 2009)
*There's A Fist Dunked In Blood
Beating In My Chest* (Epic Rites
Press 2010)
We're No Butchers (Epic Rites
Press 2011)
Death Is Dead (Epic Rites Press
2012)
Heart For Brains (Epic Rites
Press 2014)
Not Much Left For You To Stab
(Tree Killer Ink, 2014)
An Ax For The Frozen Sea (Epic
Rites Press 2015)
The Skeleton Sutras (Epic Rites
Press 2016)

www.ingramcontent.com/pod-product-compliance
Lightning Source LLC
Chambersburg PA
CBHW060950050426
42337CB00052B/3406